BATTLEFIELDS ACROSS AMERICA

YORKTOWN

MICHAEL WEBER

Twenty-First Century Books

A Division of Henry Holt and Company

New York

Twenty-First Century Books
A Division of Henry Holt and Company, Inc.
115 West 18th Street
New York, New York 10011

Henry Holt® and colophon are registered trademarks of Henry Holt and Company, Inc.
Publishers since 1866

©1997 by Blackbirch Graphics, Inc.
First Edition
5 4 3 2 1
Published in Canada by Fitzhenry & Whiteside Ltd.
195 Allstate Parkway, Markham, Ontario L3R 4T8

Printed in the United States of America on acid free paper ∞.

Created and produced in association with Blackbirch Graphics, Inc.

Photo Credits
Cover: Courtesy of the Jamestown-Yorktown Foundation; pages 4, 6, 10, 13, 14, 15, 17, 18, 23, 25, 32, 35, 37, 42, 44: North Wind Pictures; page 8: Library of Congress; page 24: Blackbirch Press, Inc.; pages 48, 50, 53: Virginia Tourism Corporation; pages 51, 54, 55: Colonial Williamsburg Foundation; page 57: Mount Vernon Ladies' Association.

All maps by Bob Italiano/©Blackbirch Graphics, Inc.

Library of Congress Cataloging-in-Publication Data
Weber, Michael, 1945-
Yorktown/Michael Weber—1st. ed.
p. cm.—(Battlefields across America)
Includes bibliographical references and index.
Summary: Focuses on the last major battle of the American Revolution after which the British forces under General Cornwallis surrendered to the Americans in October 1781.
ISBN 0-8050-5226-7
1. Yorktown (Va.)—History—Siege, 1781—Juvenile literature. [1. Yorktown (Va.)—History—Siege, 1781. 2. United States—History—Revolution, 1775-1783.] I Title. II. Series.
e241.Y6W43   1997
973.3'37—dc21   97-23371
    CIP
    AC

CONTENTS

THE AMERICAN REVOLUTION:
AMERICA'S WAR FOR INDEPENDENCE

In 1776, the 13 British colonies that had been settled in North America declared themselves an independent nation—the United States of America. To make independence a reality, however, the new nation had to fight a long and difficult war against Great Britain. That war is known as the American Revolution.

The American colonists were strong and self-reliant people. Although loyal to the British King, they believed (as did some citizens of England) that they had the right to govern themselves, select their own leaders, write their own laws, and determine their own taxes.

The Causes of the Revolution

In 1763, after winning a lengthy war with France (1756–1763), Britain acquired nearly all the French territories in North America. As a result, Britain's North American empire grew to include all of Canada in the north, the lands west of the Appalachian Mountains all the way to the Mississippi River, and the lands south of Georgia to the tip of Florida. This war, however, also cost Britain a great deal of money, and led to conflict with the North American colonies.

One problem occurred when Parliament sent soldiers to the colonies (adding to the number that were already there) to defend the vast British empire against possible Native American attacks. The Americans had never seen such a large army in peacetime, and many feared that the soldiers might interfere with their freedom. They also resented having to pay all costs of maintaining the troops.

Then in 1763, England's king, George III, issued a proclamation that prohibited colonists from moving west over the Appalachian Mountains. This law was intended to prevent conflict between the colonists and the Native Americans living in the new territories. Many Americans,

< 5 >

The Stamp Act of 1765 was protested throughout the colonies.

however, wanted to own land across the Appalachians and resented this restriction.

King George and Parliament also imposed a series of new taxes in the colonies on common items such as sugar, glass, newspapers, tea—and even playing cards. Some of this tax money was used for the salaries of British officials in the colonies who formerly had been paid by the local, elected colonial assemblies. These British officials were given more authority as well. They now had the right to search homes and warehouses for goods they suspected had been smuggled to avoid taxation. The colonists were horrified that government officials had the power to enter their homes without warning. To enforce these new tax laws, the British government created new courts in the colonies. Cases were tried before judges appointed in Britain and without juries of local citizens.

The Americans Protest

As a result of these British actions, many American colonists feared they were losing their right to self-government. A young Boston lawyer named James Otis spoke out against the 1765 tax law called the Stamp Act. He claimed that it broke "the unchangeable, unwritten code of Heaven" by which people should have complete control over their own property. Since the colonists were not

< 7 >

allowed to vote for members of Parliament, they did not think it fair that they should be taxed by Parliament. "Taxation without representation is tyranny," said Otis.[1]

Britain responded to some of the colonists' protests. In 1766, for example, Parliament repealed the Stamp Act. It passed a new law the same year, however, called the Declaratory Act, which gave Parliament the right to tax and make decisions for the British colonies "in all cases whatsoever."[2]

A few years later, Parliament imposed additional taxes in the colonies. Opposition to these taxes was particularly strong in Massachusetts, where a number of violent incidents occurred between British soldiers and American colonists.

A Crisis Over Tea

On the night of December 16, 1773, a group of Massachusetts men staged a protest against regulations that favored English tea merchants. Under cover of darkness they boarded ships in Boston Harbor that were owned by the British East India Company. Partially disguised as Native Americans, the colonists threw hundreds of chests of tea overboard. Word of this dramatic act of defiance—called the Boston Tea Party—spread throughout the colonies. For many Americans, this protest marked a turning point in their attitude toward the British government—they would no longer tolerate British tyranny.

King George and Parliament reacted angrily to the tea incident and were determined to punish the people of Massachusetts. In 1774, Parliament passed a harsh set of laws called the Coercive Acts (coercive means intending to bring about something by force or threat of force). Boston Harbor was ordered closed until the colonists paid for the ruined tea. Food and other supplies that normally arrived by ship could not be delivered to the colony. In addition, King George assumed almost complete control over the

< 8 >

government of Massachusetts. The Coercive Acts also forbade town meetings, which were a cherished, traditional form of self-government in New England. As a final insult, Bostonians were forced to shelter British soldiers—the hated "redcoats"—in their own homes.

The Continental Congresses and the Outbreak of Fighting

The colonists were outraged by these British laws, and renamed them the Intolerable Acts. All across America, people decided that it was time to take action against the British government. In September 1774, a total of 55 delegates from the colonies met in Philadelphia in the First Continental Congress—the first political body to represent the 13 American colonies. Among the delegates were Samuel Adams and John Adams from Massachusetts, and Patrick Henry and George Washington from Virginia.

Patrick Henry, a Virginia delegate, addresses the First Continental Congress.

The Continental Congress called for a repeal of the hated laws and for a colonial boycott (refusal to buy) of all British goods. The Congress also asked that each colony form militia— groups of men trained for military service and ready to fight in emergencies. If war broke out, the colonies would be able to defend themselves. The British began preparing

< 9 >

for conflict as well. King George III told Parliament that "blows must decide" who would control America, and so Parliament sent more troops to Massachusetts.[3]

Lexington and Concord

On April 19, 1775, General Thomas Gage ordered 700 British troops to "seize and destroy all the artillery and ammunition you can find" around Boston.[4] But the Massachusetts militia had been alerted and were ready. Before sunrise, Paul Revere and other Americans had crisscrossed the countryside on horseback with the warning, "The British are coming!" Fighting soon broke out in two towns near Boston—Lexington and Concord. The American Revolution had begun.

Congress Creates an Army and Appoints Washington Its Commander

In June 1775, delegates from all 13 colonies met in Philadelphia for the Second Continental Congress. Again, some of the most important men in America were present—John and Samuel Adams, Patrick Henry, and George Washington. There were also several distinguished new delegates, including Benjamin Franklin from Pennsylvania and Thomas Jefferson from Virginia.

Along with deciding certain practical matters—such as providing for the printing of money and the founding of a post office—the Second Continental Congress authorized the creation of an American army—the Continental Army. This was necessary so that the war could be fought in a more organized way than with only the local militia units. The Congress chose George Washington to command the new army. Washington, who had served in Britain's war with France, had more military experience than most Americans at the time. Washington accepted the post and offered to serve without pay.

< 10 >

America Declares Its Independence

In March 1776, the British vacated Boston, and the focus of the war turned toward New York. Meanwhile, Congress debated a momentous issue: Should the 13 colonies declare themselves an independent nation, or should the colonies remain possessions of the British empire?

On July 9, 1776, the Declaration of Independence was read aloud to General Washington (on the white horse) and the newly formed Continental Army.

On June 7, 1776, the Virginia delegate Richard Henry Lee proposed "that these United Colonies are, and of right ought to be, free and independent States...and that all political connection between them and the State of Great Britain is, and ought to be, totally dissolved."[5] While Congress considered Lee's proposal, a committee was appointed to draft a document declaring the new nation's independence. The committee chose Thomas Jefferson to write this "Declaration of Independence."

Not all delegates, however, supported the idea of independence. Some still hoped that the conflict between the colonies and Britain would be resolved. Others

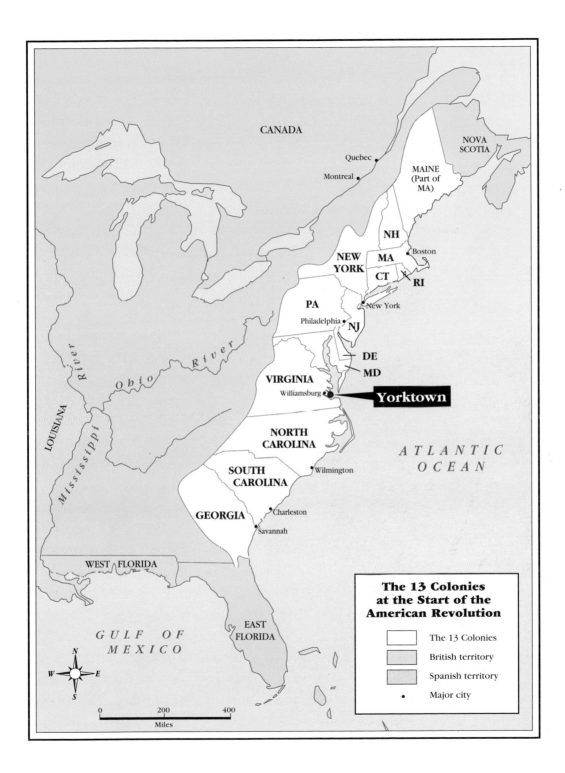

CANADA

Quebec

Montreal

NOVA
SCOTIA

MAINE
(Part of
MA)

NH

NEW
YORK

MA

Boston

CT

RI

PA

New York

Philadelphia

NJ

DE

MD

VIRGINIA

Williamsburg

Yorktown

Ohio River

Mississippi River

LOUISIANA

NORTH
CAROLINA

SOUTH
CAROLINA

Wilmington

GEORGIA

Charleston

Savannah

ATLANTIC
OCEAN

WEST FLORIDA

EAST
FLORIDA

GULF OF
MEXICO

N
W   E
S

0   200   400

Miles

The 13 Colonies
at the Start of the
American Revolution

The 13 Colonies

British territory

Spanish territory

• Major city

< 12 >

argued that Americans wanted a separate nation, and that since the war had begun, independence was already a fact. After some debate, Congress approved Lee's proposal on July 2. The delegates then considered Jefferson's draft of the Declaration of Independence. They made some changes to the document, after which it was ratified (approved) on July 4, 1776. It was then signed by John Hancock, the president of Congress, and Charles Thomson, the secretary. The remaining signatures were added to the declaration on August 2, after it was printed on official parchment paper.

The Course of the War Through 1780

In a letter to his wife, John Adams wrote, "We shall have a long, obstinate and bloody war to go through."[6] Unlike Adams, however, most Americans did not anticipate a lengthy or difficult war.

The British also expected to win the war quickly. After all, Britain had the world's most powerful navy and an experienced, well-equipped army, in addition to being a wealthier nation. Moreover, not all Americans supported independence. Some colonists, known as Loyalists or Tories, remained loyal to King George.

Although the American army was inexperienced and short of weapons and ammunition, it had a number of advantages over the British army. The American soldiers believed strongly in fighting for their liberty and defending their land—morale was high. Because America was a large country, the British would need to send thousands of soldiers to fight the war. Those soldiers would have to travel a distance of some 3,000 miles across the Atlantic Ocean. Short of men, the British were forced to hire troops from the armies of several German princes. The Americans called these soldiers Hessians, since many of them came from a region in Germany called Hesse-Cassel.

< 13 >

Defeats, Victories, and an Important Alliance

Although the British won many battles of the American Revolution, the Americans won strategically important victories. In October 1777, an American victory at Saratoga, New York, changed the course of the war. There, an American army led by General Horatio Gates defeated a British force under General John Burgoyne's command. The British were forced to surrender. This defeat ruined a grand plan to divide the United States in two. Even more importantly, the battle at Saratoga led to a crucial alliance between the Americans and the French government.

When news of the battle reached France, King Louis XVI and his ministers officially recognized the independence of the United States. In February 1778, an American delegation led by Benjamin Franklin went to Paris to sign a treaty of alliance with France. The French government agreed to supply the United States with money, equipment, and soldiers, as well as a powerful navy.

General Burgoyne (left) surrendered his sword to General Gates after the Americans defeated the British at Saratoga in October 1777. Gates returned it immediately.

The two British generals chiefly concerned with the Battle of Yorktown did not get along well. Both men preferred communicating directly with London and neither one fully confided his plans and expectations to the other. Their rivalry hurt the British war effort.

Sir Henry Clinton was born in Newfoundland in 1730 and grew up in New York, where his father was the British governor for a time. He went to England in 1751 and there joined the army. Clinton's wife died in 1772 after they had been married for five years. The loss profoundly affected Clinton. He became moody and often quarreled with his colleagues. When Cornwallis was defeated by Washington at Princeton in 1776, Clinton remarked that Cornwallis had shown "the most consummate ignorance I ever heard of [in] any officer."[7]

Clinton became commander of all the British armies in America in 1778, succeeding Sir William Howe. From his headquarters in New York,

Sir Henry Clinton

Word of the French alliance did not reach America, however, until the spring of 1778. Some of the promised aid took even longer to arrive. In the meantime, Washington and his army struggled through the bitter winter at Valley Forge, 21 miles west of Philadelphia. The British had taken control of Philadelphia in October 1777. The American soldiers suffered from shortages of

Clinton entertained lavishly with parties and concerts.

Clinton returned to his home in England in 1782. Blamed for Britain's defeat in the war, he wrote an account of the 1781 events at Yorktown in order to defend his reputation. Clinton died in 1795 while serving as governor of Gibraltar.

Lord Charles Cornwallis was born in 1738 to a wealthy and well-known family. At the age of 18, he entered the army—despite the fact that he was blind in one eye from a hockey injury. While he was a member of Parliament, Cornwallis strongly opposed the new taxes that had so angered the American colonists.

Like Clinton, Cornwallis served during the Revolution under Sir William Howe in New York, New Jersey, and Pennsylvania. More popular than Clinton in England, Cornwallis tried

Lord Charles Cornwallis

to ignore the general and deal directly with the government in London.

After the Revolution, Cornwallis served with great success in India and in Ireland. He died while in India in 1805.

even the most basic and necessary requirements—food, clothing, and shelter. Washington reported to Congress that he had nearly 3,000 men "unfit for duty, because barefoot and other wise naked."[8] An army doctor at Valley Forge asked, "Why are we sent here to freeze and starve?"[9] Yet the army managed to survive the long and difficult winter.

< 16 >

In June 1778, the British army left Philadelphia and went to New York City. Sir Henry Clinton took command of the British forces from General William Howe. Washington's army pursued the British troops and established camp north of the city, at White Plains.

The War in the South

During the remaining years of the American Revolution, most of the battles were fought in the South. The British, who had not met with success in the northern colonies, turned their attention to the South. They believed that Loyalist feeling there was strong, especially in Georgia, North Carolina, and South Carolina.

In 1779, British troops captured Savannah, Georgia, and then overran most of the state. In 1780, British forces besieged Charleston, South Carolina, which surrendered in May. Thousands of American soldiers and sailors were taken prisoner in the worst American defeat of the war. A member of Parliament declared, "We look on America as at our feet."[10]

At this point, Clinton put Sir Charles Cornwallis in charge of all British forces in the South. The Continental Congress sent General Gates to fight Cornwallis with an army composed of militia units and regulars (foot soldiers) from Washington's forces. Gates attacked at Camden, South Carolina, in August 1780, but was badly defeated and his forces were scattered.

Nevertheless, the British had overestimated Loyalist support in the South. Their attempt to invade central North Carolina in September failed when frontier militia killed 1,000 Loyalist soldiers at Kings Mountain. As British troops marched through the countryside, their supply lines were frequently attacked by small bands of American soldiers. These men would appear suddenly, strike their blows, and then disappear before a full-scale battle could be fought. Today this kind of fighting is called guerrilla warfare.

Troops attempted to defend Savannah, Georgia, from the British in October 1779, but they were defeated.

At Washington's urging, the Continental Congress sent Nathanael Greene to replace General Gates in October. Under Greene's leadership, the American army fought Cornwallis's men so vigorously that, in April 1781, after several battles, Cornwallis withdrew to Wilmington, North Carolina. He wrote to a British officer, "I am quite tired of marching about the country.... If we mean an offensive war in America, we must abandon New York and bring our whole force into Virginia."[11] Later that month, Cornwallis marched with his army to Virginia without consulting Clinton. To Clinton, this move was "inexcusable."[12]

THE BATTLE OF YORKTOWN:
THE CLIMAX OF THE AMERICAN REVOLUTION

By the spring of 1781, the American Revolution had been going on for six years. No end was in sight. The soldiers on both sides were tired of the war and in low spirits.

The British occupied New York City; Charleston, South Carolina; and Savannah, Georgia; and had troops in Virginia. But they were no closer to ending the American rebellion than they had been in 1775.

From New York, General Clinton wrote to government officials in London "of the utter impossibility of prosecuting the war in this country without re-inforcements." Clinton claimed that he needed thousands of additional troops "to subdue this formidable rebellion."[1]

The Road to Yorktown

Washington, and the main force of the Continental Army—only about 3,500 men at this time—were camped along the Hudson River north of New York City. The army was again short of food, clothing, and ammunition. The soldiers had not been paid, since Congress had no money. Naturally, this discouraged men from enlisting. Even more problematic were the mutinies that occurred within the American army in 1781. Pennsylvania troops on duty in New Jersey killed an American officer. They then began marching toward Philadelphia to demand their pay from Congress. Although the troops didn't reach Philadelphia, they were persuaded by several government officials to return to their camps. The trouble spread to a few other regiments, and Washington was forced to send more reliable troops to keep the men in line. Two soldiers were executed for their crimes.

Although three years had passed since the alliance had been made with France, it had not produced all the benefits hoped for by the Americans. In 1780, a division of French soldiers—more than 4,000

< 19 >

< 20 >

men—had sailed into Newport's harbor, in Rhode Island, but had seen little battle. A promised second division had not yet arrived.

Marquis de Lafayette, a young French nobleman, had come to America in 1777 to help in the fight for liberty. Lafayette returned briefly to France to plead the American cause. He told the French government that the Americans could not defeat Britain, with its powerful navy that enabled soldiers to be moved wherever they were needed, unaided. France, said Lafayette, should provide the American cause with "naval superiority for the next campaign."[2]

The Continental Congress also appealed to France for more aid. Washington wrote in April 1781, "We are at the end of our tether and now or never our deliverance must come."[3] A month later, he said that America needed "ships, land troops, and money" from France.[4] A few more months would pass, however, before any further help from France finally arrived.

Cornwallis and the War in Virginia

On May 20, 1781, Cornwallis and his army reached Petersburg, Virginia. British troops had already arrived in the state. Benedict Arnold—the American general who went over to the British side in September 1780—had been sent by Clinton to Virginia with 1,200 men to do as much damage as possible. They landed in January and were later reinforced with 2,000 more soldiers. Arnold's men caused so much trouble that Washington dispatched General Lafayette with 1,200 soldiers to stop them. Lafayette arrived in Virginia in April. Later in the spring, General Anthony Wayne and others joined him, increasing his forces to 4,000.

When Cornwallis arrived in Virginia, the 8,300 men under his command outnumbered those under Lafayette. The French general could do little more than watch the British movements from a distance. One of Cornwallis's officers, Banastre Tarleton, and a group

< 21 >

of cavalry (soldiers who fight on horseback) raided Charlottesville, then serving as Virginia's capital. Tarleton captured seven Virginia legislators, one of whom was Daniel Boone (then a colonel), and came within minutes of seizing the governor, Thomas Jefferson.

At this point, however, the British made a major strategic mistake by ordering Cornwallis to take up a position on the coast where he could easily become trapped. There, he was told to establish a naval base. In June and July, Cornwallis received a series of confusing orders from the government in London and from Clinton in New York—they arrived out of sequence. Clinton's order came first, requesting that Cornwallis ship several thousand troops to New York as reinforcements against a possible attack. Cornwallis accordingly started marching toward Portsmouth, where his troops would be able to board ships bound for New York. Cornwallis then received new orders, which canceled the earlier ones. These orders told him to position his troops near the Chesapeake Bay on the York River.

Cornwallis decided to make his base at Yorktown on the peninsula. This tobacco port could accommodate large ships, and could also serve as a base for land operations. Cornwallis arrived there with his army early in August and began building fortifications around the town, and at Gloucester Point on the opposite shore.

The Plan to Trap Cornwallis

Following Cornwallis's army from a cautious distance, Lafayette moved the American forces to a place near Williamsburg, 12 miles west of Yorktown. Lafayette now saw the possibility of trapping the British on the peninsula. He wrote to Washington, "Should a French fleet now come...the British army would, I think, be ours."[5]

Washington had been keeping track of the situation as well. In May, he met with Comte de Rochambeau, the French general

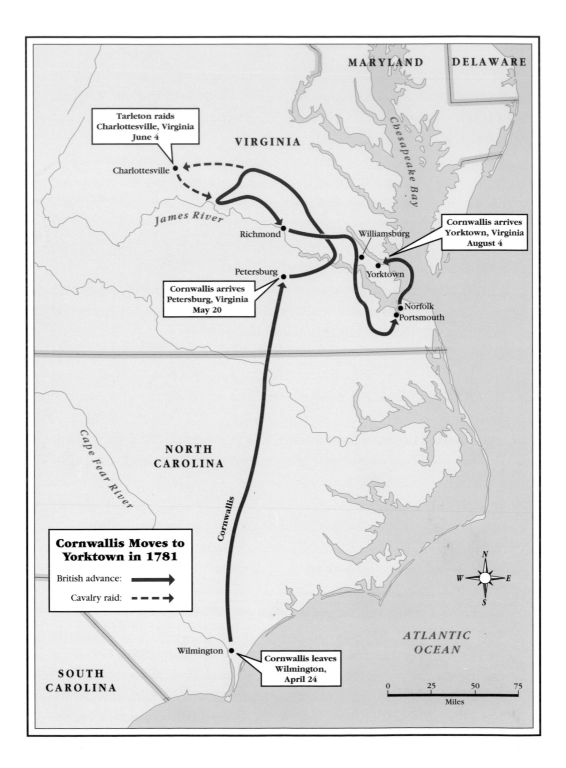

MARYLAND   DELAWARE

Tarleton raids
Charlottesville, Virginia
June 4

VIRGINIA

Chesapeake Bay

Charlottesville

James River

Richmond

Williamsburg

Cornwallis arrives
Yorktown, Virginia
August 4

Yorktown

Petersburg

Cornwallis arrives
Petersburg, Virginia
May 20

Norfolk
Portsmouth

Cape Fear River

NORTH
CAROLINA

Cornwallis

**Cornwallis Moves to
Yorktown in 1781**

British advance:

Cavalry raid:

N
W   *E*
S

*ATLANTIC
OCEAN*

Wilmington

Cornwallis leaves
Wilmington,
April 24

SOUTH
CAROLINA

0   25   50   75
Miles

whose troops were encamped in Rhode Island, to discuss a joint operation against the British. Rochambeau told Washington that France had agreed to send a large fleet to America, commanded by Admiral François De Grasse. In June, the French army marched from Newport to join the Continental Army camped along the Hudson. Watching the Americans, a French observer wrote, "It is incredible that soldiers composed of men of every age, even of children of fifteen, whites and blacks, almost naked, unpaid, and rather poorly fed, can march so well and stand fire so steadfastly." He attributed this to "the calm and calculated measures of General Washington....Everyone regards him as his father and friend."[6]

Washington (right) and Rochambeau met in Connecticut to discuss a joint strategy against the British.

Washington's initial strategy was to attack the British in New York City. However, on August 14, Washington learned that Admiral De Grasse was sailing from the West Indies to Chesapeake Bay with a large fleet of warships and 3,000 soldiers, but would remain there only until October 14. Without French naval support to attack New York City, Washington and Rochambeau resolved on a bold plan: They would hurry south to trap Cornwallis in Virginia.

Unlike their British counterparts, the American and French generals at the Battle of Yorktown respected each other and cooperated well with one another.

George Washington was one of the greatest Americans of his day. He was born in Virginia in 1732. Washington's father, a wealthy planter, died when George was only 11 years old. The boy was raised by his elder half-brother, Lawrence.

Washington joined the Virginia militia and in 1755 became commander of the militia sent into western Pennsylvania early in Britain's war with France. Later in that war, Washington served as an aide to the chief British general, Edward Braddock. When the Revolution began in 1775, Washington was one of the most experienced military men in America and was widely respected for his judgment and character.

After the Revolution, Washington presided over the Constitutional Convention in 1787. He was unanimously elected the first president of the United States in 1789. Washington died in 1799, after serving as president for two terms. Thomas Jefferson, who knew Washington well, said he was "in every sense of the words, a wise, a good, and a great man."[7]

Marquis de Lafayette's full name was Marie Joseph Paul Gilbert du Motier, the Marquis de Lafayette. He was born into a wealthy family in 1757 and entered the French army in 1771 at the age of 14. Six years later, he resigned from the army and secretly came to America. "The moment I heard of America," he wrote, "I loved her; the moment I knew she was fighting for freedom, I burned with a desire of bleeding for her."[8] Shortly after he arrived in America, Congress made Lafayette a major-general.

Lafayette became a great favorite of George Washington. When he was seriously wounded in battle in 1777, Washington told Lafayette's doctor,

George Washington

"Treat him as if he were my son, for I love him as if he were."[9]

Lafayette went back to France after the American Revolution, returning to America for a brief visit in 1784. He played a prominent part in the French Revolution and in the subsequent history of France. Lafayette visited America for the last time in 1824-25. He died in 1834.

Comte de Rochambeau, the commander of the French army in America, was born to a wealthy family in 1725. His full name was Jean Baptiste Donatien de Vimeur, Comte de Rochambeau. He first studied for the priesthood, but entered the army instead in 1742.

A good-humored man, Rochambeau willingly subordinated himself to Washington, although he always spoke his mind. When he first arrived in America in 1780, he wrote to Washington, "The commands of the King [of France]…place me under the orders of Your Excellency. I come, wholly obedient and with the zeal and the veneration which I have for you and for the remarkable talents you have displayed in sustaining a war which will always be memorable."[10] In 1783, Rochambeau returned to France. He narrowly escaped execution during the French Revolution.

Marquis de Lafayette

Comte de Rochambeau

< 26 >

The Americans and French Move South

The plan to trap Cornwallis was quite a gamble. Yorktown was 450 miles away. The American and French armies would need to travel much of the way on foot and then sail across the Chesapeake Bay. Their heavy guns would be transported by sea, carried by a small French fleet sailing from Newport. Food, tents, and boats for the troops all would need to be provided. But what if Clinton's large army blocked their route? What if a British fleet prevented the ships from leaving Newport or Admiral De Grasse's fleet from reaching the Chesapeake? What if Cornwallis managed to defeat Lafayette's army and leave Yorktown before the Americans and the French were able to arrive?

Washington, with only a portion of his army and the entire French force, started off during the last week in August. The armies crossed the river and marched south through New Jersey and on to Philadelphia. To deceive Clinton into thinking he was moving against New York, Washington ordered ovens built in Chatham, New Jersey—supposedly to bake bread for troops attacking New York. A bridge leading in the direction of the city was repaired as well. For a while, even the American and French soldiers did not know their destination. "We do not know the object of our march, and are in perfect ignorance whether we are going against New York, or whether we are going to Virginia," said one American.[11]

For a while, Clinton *was* fooled. On August 30, the day Washington entered Philadelphia, the British commander wrote to Cornwallis, "Washington's force still remains in the neighborhood of Chatham and I do not hear that he has yet detached to the southward."[12] A few days later, Clinton realized what was happening. He wrote to Cornwallis that Washington was heading south and promised to send reinforcements.

< 27 >

Good News

On September 2, the American soldiers entered Philadelphia. The French troops followed over the next two days and paraded through the city.

As he watched the parading troops, Washington had much to worry about. He was concerned about the details of supplying the two armies and transporting them to Virginia. The American soldiers still had not been paid. And, as he wrote to Lafayette, "I am distressed beyond expression to know what has become of the Comte De Grasse and for fear that the English fleet, by occupying the Chesapeake...may frustrate all our flattering prospects."[13]

Washington left for Virginia ahead of the armies, to spend a few days at his home in Mount Vernon. As he was riding near Chester, Pennsylvania, a man on horseback galloped up to him with a message. After reading its contents, Washington's whole expression changed. The large French fleet under De Grasse had arrived in Chesapeake Bay near Yorktown on August 31! A French officer who was at the scene near Chester wrote that Washington's "naturally cold" expression changed. "I have never seen a man moved by a greater or sincerer joy."[14]

From Philadelphia, the American and French armies continued on foot through Delaware and into Maryland. There, at various points along the Chesapeake Bay, they boarded boats and set sail for Jamestown on the James River, 25 miles from Yorktown. There also, to their great joy, the Americans were paid. A large French loan had finally come through, and kegs full of silver coins were delivered to the troops. In the words of a major from New York, "This day will be famous in the annals of history."[15] Because they were not issued army uniforms, the soldiers spent their pay on clothing, as well as food, liquor, and entertainment. Some men also sent money home to their families.

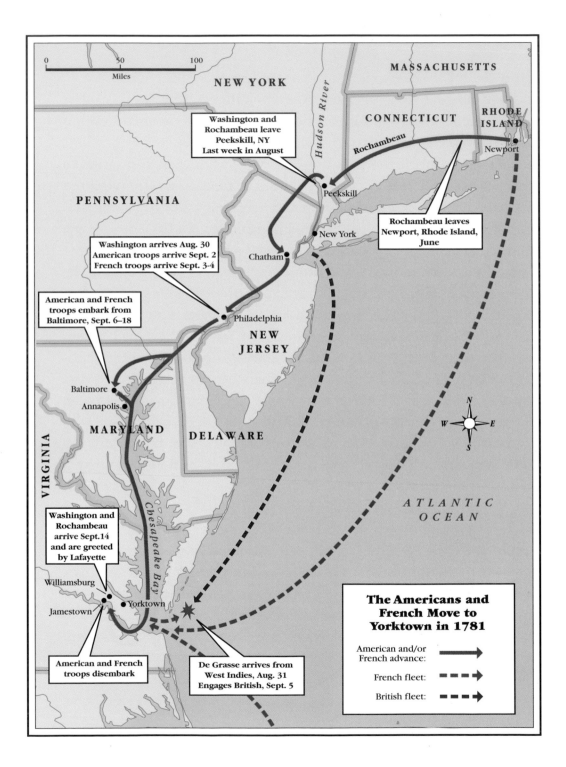

The Americans and French Move to Yorktown in 1781

American and/or French advance: →

French fleet: ▪▪▪→

British fleet: ▪▪▪→

Washington and Rochambeau leave Peekskill, NY Last week in August

Rochambeau leaves Newport, Rhode Island, June

Washington arrives Aug. 30 American troops arrive Sept. 2 French troops arrive Sept. 3-4

American and French troops embark from Baltimore, Sept. 6–18

Washington and Rochambeau arrive Sept.14 and are greeted by Lafayette

American and French troops disembark

De Grasse arrives from West Indies, Aug. 31 Engages British, Sept. 5

< 29 >

Washington continued his journey to Virginia on horseback, and both he and Rochambeau arrived at Williamsburg on September 14. Lafayette—who had just celebrated his 24th birthday—waited with his troops to greet the two generals. An onlooker recorded that as Lafayette approached Washington, he "opened both his arms as wide as he could reach, and caught the General round his body, hugged him as close as it was possible, and absolutely kissed him from ear to ear."[16] That night, Washington heard the good news—the French fleet under De Grasse's command had defeated a British fleet off the Virginia coast on September 5. The British fleet had sailed from New York and arrived on September 5 to find De Grasse waiting. De Grasse's fleet was blockading the Chesapeake Bay and the York River, preventing any rescue of Cornwallis by sea.

By September 26, 1781, all the American and French forces had reached Williamsburg. Earlier in September, 3,000 French soldiers commanded by Marquis Claude Marie de Saint-Simon had come ashore from De Grasse's fleet at Jamestown, near Williamsburg. Referring to Cornwallis's situation, General Wayne happily reported to Lafayette, "Every door is shut."[17]

Yorktown —The Setting

Yorktown is located on a peninsula that juts into the Chesapeake Bay between the James and York Rivers. The port of Yorktown was built on the northern side of the peninsula, on a bluff overlooking the narrowest part of the York River. Directly across the river, one-half mile away, was Gloucester Point. Twelve miles up the peninsula, to the west, was Williamsburg, the former capital of Virginia. (In 1780, the capital was moved to Richmond.) Just south of Williamsburg, on the James River, was Jamestown, the site of the first permanent English settlement in America.

< 30 >

Immediately to the west of Yorktown was a ravine and a swampy area where Yorktown Creek flowed into the York River. Wormley Creek joined the river to the southeast. The land immediately facing the town, however, was flat and sandy. Since there was no high ground on this land, it provided no advantages for the British defenders.

The Two Sides Compared

Cornwallis had almost 8,300 men under his command at Yorktown and at Gloucester Point. They were the most experienced British soldiers in America. Included in this number were about 2,000 Hessians and 100 Loyalists from North Carolina.

When all the American and French forces had arrived on the peninsula, however, they far outnumbered the British. All together, there were nearly 17,600 American and French troops under Washington's command. They also had more heavy artillery (large, manned, and mounted firearms that were all classed as cannons in the 18th century) than the British. This was a rare occurrence in the American Revolution.

The Americans had about 9,000 soldiers, including some 3,500 Virginia militiamen commanded by General Thomas Nelson, Jr. Washington divided his 5,500 Continental troops into three groups—one under Lafayette, one under General Benjamin Lincoln, and the third under Baron von Steuben. Von Steuben had come from Prussia, in Germany, in 1778. He had helped to train the Continental Army at Valley Forge. General Henry Knox commanded the American artillery.

The French land forces numbered nearly 8,600 men. In addition to Rochambeau's 4,800 troops were the 3,000 men who were under Saint-Simon's command from De Grasse's fleet and 800 French seamen. In addition, De Grasse had about 16,900 naval personnel.

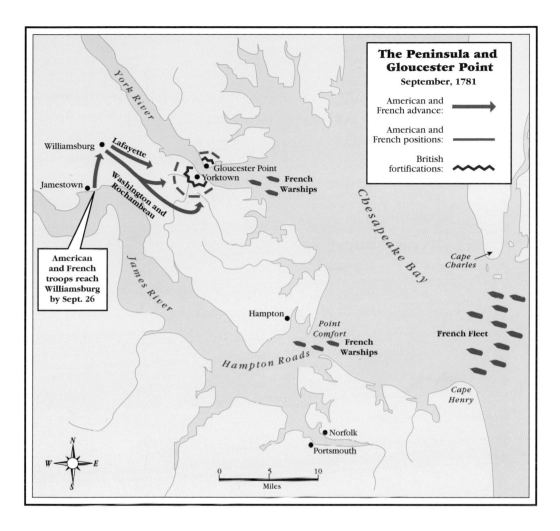

The Peninsula and Gloucester Point
September, 1781

American and French advance:

American and French positions:

British fortifications:

American and French troops reach Williamsburg by Sept. 26

York River

Williamsburg

Lafayette

Washington and Rochambeau

Jamestown

Gloucester Point

Yorktown

French Warships

Chesapeake Bay

Cape Charles

James River

Hampton

Point Comfort

French Warships

French Fleet

Hampton Roads

Cape Henry

Norfolk

Portsmouth

N W E S

0   5   10

Miles

A significant number of men on both sides, however, were sick with malaria and other illnesses. Lafayette had been sick just prior to Washington's arrival. Saint-Simon and many of his men had become ill after they landed. About one third of Cornwallis's forces were too ill to take part in the battle at Yorktown.

The British Dig In

After their arrival in August, Cornwallis's troops, and 2,000 runaway slaves who had been promised freedom by the British, had begun digging trenches and building fortifications around Yorktown.

< 32 >

Working under conditions of extreme heat and humidity, they saw no need to hurry during the first few weeks. The men soon became alarmed, however, in early September when the French soldiers from De Grasse's fleet landed. The digging was speeded up so much that a Hessian soldier complained, "We hardly had time for eating."[18] Expecting reinforcements from Clinton in New York, Cornwallis made no attempt to attack the American and French armies and fight his way up the peninsula. He wrote to Clinton, "If I had not hopes

This British ship on the York River was destroyed by French artillery fire.

< 33 >

of Relief, I would rather risk an Action [battle] than defend my half-finished Works. But as you...promised every Exertion to assist me, I do not think myself justifiable in putting the fate of the War on so desperate an Attempt."[19]

A few days later, the British heard gunfire coming from the sea. They did not realize at first that what they were hearing was the naval battle in which the French fleet under De Grasse had driven off the British fleet. The men began to sense that they were in serious trouble. "A fatal storm," wrote one officer, is "ready now almost to burst on our heads."[20]

The British built two lines of fortifications for defense. These consisted of trenches and strongholds, or redoubts (earthen forts), that were reinforced with logs and branches. Artillery was placed in the redoubts. The British fortification known as the inner defense line surrounded Yorktown and was about 1.5 miles long. In the outer defense line, further away from the town, there were three crucial redoubts: On the west, near Yorktown Creek, was the Fusilier's Redoubt, named for the unit that was posted there; on the other side, southeast of town, were Redoubts 9 and 10. Other portions of the outer defenses blocked the road from Williamsburg to Yorktown. Cornwallis had also stationed troops under Lieutenant Thomas Dundas on Gloucester Point, across the river. Minor defenses were built there as well.

The Americans and French Take Up Their Positions

At dawn on September 28, the American and French troops began moving out of Williamsburg toward Yorktown. The day was already hot. The Marquis de Saint-Simon was so ill that he had to be carried on a stretcher. At about 3:00 P.M., the soldiers came within sight of the town—and some of the British outer defenses. Washington came up to view the scene. He knew the area fairly

< 34 >

well, having visited Yorktown often as a young man. Washington ordered 1,500 Virginia militia under General George Weedon's command to hem the British in at Gloucester Point. Later, the militiamen were reinforced by French cavalry and marines, and all were put under the command of the Marquis de Choisy.

Outside Yorktown, the French forces took up positions on the left side, with the Americans on the right. On the morning of September 30, the American and French soldiers were surprised to find that the British had abandoned some of their outer defenses along the road to Williamsburg. Cornwallis had received a message from Clinton saying that his reinforcements soon would leave New York. Until they arrived, Cornwallis decided to form a tighter defense around his inner defense line. The Americans quickly occupied the abandoned positions. They now had an opportunity to build their own defenses closer to the British, from which they could safely bombard Yorktown.

That afternoon, Washington issued a statement. "The present moment," he said, "will decide American independence.... The passive conduct of the enemy argues his weakness.... The liberties of America and the honour of the Allied Arms are in our hands."[21]

The Siege of Yorktown

The battle of Yorktown was a siege. In a siege, an attacking army surrounds a town, city, or another army in order to prevent food and other supplies from reaching its inhabitants or members. The attackers also bombard the town with artillery in an attempt to force it to surrender. From inside the city walls, the defenders try to destroy the attackers' artillery with fire from their own guns.

As the British soldiers had done around Yorktown, the American and French forces constructed fortifications and trenches for their artillery outside the town. Preparations to begin construction took almost a week. All the equipment was brought to the front lines. The heavy guns were dragged into place using long ropes. Initially, this work was done by hand because most of the army's horses did not arrive until October 4. To speed up the work, the horses of Washington and other officers were used to haul artillery. Many soldiers were in the woods cutting branches to use in building the fortifications. While the troops worked, they came under fire as the British attempted to disrupt their progress. Bullets whizzed past Washington when he came to the front lines to see how things were going.

Washington (right) and Rochambeau view the British positions from the trenches before the siege.

Tension mounted as preparations continued for what would clearly be a major battle. Soldiers from both sides began to desert, although many more British than Americans abandoned their posts. Washington issued a warning to the men under his command: "Every deserter from the American troops...will be instantly Hanged."[22]

On October 6, the weather grew dismal—it began to rain and a chilly wind began to blow. Now, with all the equipment on hand, Washington ordered the construction of a large earthwork, called a parallel, 1,000 yards from the British lines. It would be 2,000 feet long, extending from Yorktown Creek to a bluff near the river.

< 36 >

The earthwork would have many positions for artillery batteries. The work needed to be done under cover of darkness. This first parallel, also called the first siege line, was dug by 1,500 men on the night of October 6. The platforms for the cannons and the cannons themselves—18- and 24-pound cannons, a dozen mortars (a small type of cannon), and 8-inch howitzers (more powerful than mortars)—were put in place on October 8 and the morning of October 9. Lieutenant Colonel Alexander Hamilton of New York—a good friend of Washington and later the first U.S. secretary of the treasury—led the first American infantry (foot soldiers) into the parallel.

The Bombardment Begins

At 3:00 in the afternoon, on October 9, the bombardment of the British in Yorktown began. The French guns were fired first. Two hours later, the American flag was raised, signaling that the bombardment should begin from the American artillery and the remaining French batteries. Sergeant Joseph Martin of Massachusetts later recalled, "I felt a secret pride swell my heart when I saw `the Star-Spangled Banner' waving majestically in the very faces of our implacable adversaries. It appeared like an omen of success."[23]

The bombardment was highly effective. It was heavier than anything the British had yet experienced in the war. Cornwallis wrote, "The fire continued incessant from heavy cannon...until all our guns on the left were silenced, our work [fortifications] much damaged and our loss of men considerable."[24] The American and French troops fired their artillery all through the night to prevent the British from repairing their damaged positions. Johann Doehla, a Hessian soldier, wrote that "it felt like the shocks of an earthquake. One saw men lying everywhere who were mortally wounded and whose heads, arms, and legs had been shot off."[25]

The American and French armies tighten their siege of British-held Yorktown.

Around noon the next day, the British released a frail, elderly man, Thomas Nelson, along with his servant. (This practice was not unusual in the 18th century, at which time warfare was more civilized, particularly among the upper classes.) Nelson was the uncle of Thomas Nelson, Jr., the commander of the Virginia militia at Yorktown. Cornwallis had been living in Nelson's Yorktown house, near the edge of town, which had been battered in the bombardment. The released Nelson reported to Washington that the heavy gunfire had driven Cornwallis and his staff out of his house. Cornwallis was now headquartered in an earthen bunker in the terraced gardens behind Nelson's house. The British had suffered heavy losses.

Later that day, Lafayette asked Nelson, Jr., if there was a particular spot in Yorktown that the artillery gunners should target. Pointing toward a fine house in the center of town, Nelson said, "Have them fire there. It's my house."[26] Visitors to Yorktown

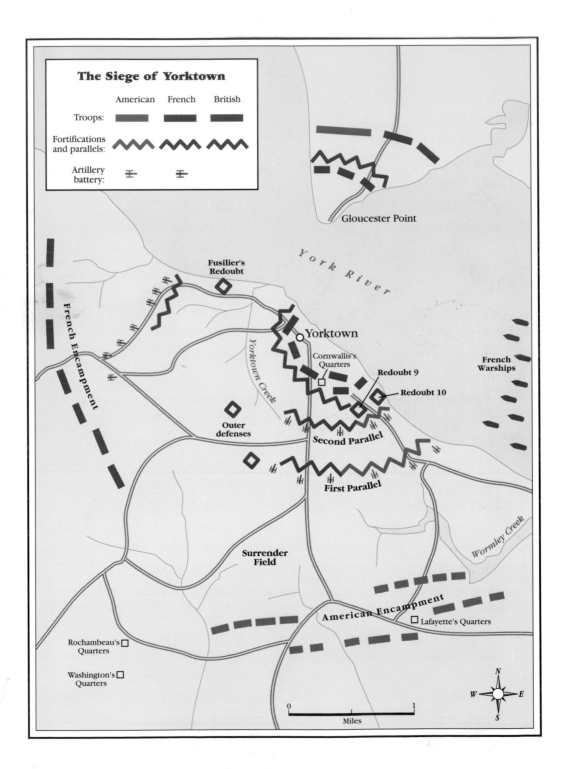

The Siege of Yorktown

American   French   British

Troops:

Fortifications
and parallels:

Artillery
battery:

Gloucester Point

York River

Fusilier's
Redoubt

French Encampment

Yorktown

Cornwallis's
Quarters

Redoubt 9

Redoubt 10

French
Warships

Outer
defenses

Second Parallel

First Parallel

Surrender
Field

American Encampment

Lafayette's Quarters

Rochambeau's
Quarters

Washington's
Quarters

Wormley Creek

Yorktown Creek

0   1
Miles

N
W   E
S

< **39** >

today can see the house, which still shows the damage in its outer walls from the American and French shells.

On October 11, Cornwallis received a message from Clinton. It was delivered by an officer whose small boat had slipped past the French blockade. The message said that Clinton was doing his best to send help. Cornwallis replied, "We cannot hope to make a very long Resistance."[27] The next day, that same officer was killed by a cannonball as he stood watching the guns firing with Cornwallis.

The Siege Tightens

As the siege progressed, Washington ordered a second parallel dug closer to the British lines, and work began on the night of October 11. British Redoubts 9 and 10 prevented the new earthwork from being extended to the river. So, on the night of October 14, Washington ordered that they be stormed, each by a 400-man force.

First, men with axes went to cut some paths through the abatis—barricades made of trees with sharp-edged branches that the British had placed before the ditches of the redoubts. The soldiers then charged the positions. American soldiers led by Colonel Alexander Hamilton attacked Redoubt 10, nearest the river. French soldiers led by Baron Antoine Charles Vioménil attacked Redoubt 9.

As the soldiers advanced, some fell into holes that had been created by the artillery bombardment. At Redoubt 10, Lieutenant John Mansfield of Connecticut, the first man over the wall, was stabbed by a British bayonet. Hamilton, a short man, climbed on another man's back to get over the wall. The redoubt and its British commander were quickly captured. The Americans lost 9 men, and 25 were wounded. Among the casualties was Sergeant William Brown of Connecticut, who became the first soldier to receive the Purple Heart medal—a U.S. military decoration awarded by the government to members of the armed forces wounded in action.

< 40 >

The French attack on Redoubt 9 was more costly. The French lost 15 men, and 77 were wounded. But eventually the Hessian and British defenders retreated. When they did so, some were mistakenly shot by their own men in the confusion. The fighting for the redoubts cost the British about 20 men, and an unknown number were wounded. Fifty British soldiers were captured.

Earthworks were built linking the captured redoubts to the second parallel, also called the second siege line, and allied artillery was moved into them.

The British Fight On

Cornwallis wrote to Clinton on October 15, "My situation now becomes very critical.... We shall soon be exposed to an assault in ruined Works, in a bad position and with weakened Numbers. I cannot recommend that the Fleet and Army should run great risque in endeavoring to save us."[28]

Cornwallis, however, was not yet ready to give up. That night, he ordered an attack on artillery batteries in the second parallel where the American and French positions were joined. Cornwallis believed that this was the weakest point in the enemy's position. The action, led by Lieutenant Robert Abercromby, began at 4:00 A.M. Several dozen men were killed or wounded on each side, but this attack had little effect on the battle's outcome. A number of guns were "spiked," or put out of action, but they were soon repaired.

On October 16, Cornwallis made a desperate move. The Hessian soldier named Doehla noted that "everybody easily saw that we could not hold out much longer in this place if we did not get help soon."[29] Several British officers had been urging Cornwallis to send the infantry across the river to Gloucester Point. There, with luck, they could defeat Choisy's forces, capture his horses, and escape toward New York. In the words of cavalry leader Tarleton,

< 41 >

"A retreat by Gloucester [Point] is the only expedient...to avert the mortification of a surrender."[30]

Cornwallis finally agreed to the plan. The soldiers who were sick and wounded would all be left behind, along with the few horses and whatever heavy guns were left. (The British had already killed 1,000 horses rather than have them starve.) Around midnight, 1,000 soldiers boarded boats and crossed the river. Cornwallis wrote to Washington asking that the abandoned men be treated kindly. As the British general prepared to depart with a second group of soldiers, a sudden storm came down the river. Two boatloads of soldiers were driven downstream and captured, and the escape attempt was abandoned. The men who had already made it across the river returned the next day and reported, "We'll never break through there. They have trenches around our whole garrison.... Nothing passes in or out."[31]

The British Surrender

On October 17, the American and French bombardment of Yorktown, now with approximately 70 guns, (which at that time in history was a large number) was heavier than ever. More and more British soldiers were being wounded. Many were still sick. Only about 3,200 men were capable of fighting, and they were exhausted. Food had been in short supply for weeks.

After inspecting the British fortifications early that morning, Cornwallis saw that they could scarcely be defended any longer. He realized that their situation was hopeless. He met with his staff and concluded, as he later wrote to Clinton, that "under all these circumstances, I thought it would have been wanton and inhuman to...sacrifice the lives of this small body of gallant soldiers."[32] The British at Yorktown would surrender.

On October 17, 1781, a young soldier marked the British army's surrender with a drumroll.

The Surrender Negotiations

In the morning on October 17, a young British soldier climbed to the top of a wall in front of the British lines. He played a drumroll, which was the signal for a conference. At first, the sounds of cannonfire drowned out the boy's drum. Gradually, however, the cannons fell silent. Ebenezer Denny of Pennsylvania called the drumroll "the most delightful music to us all."[33] A British officer then appeared, waving a white handkerchief. He carried a message from Cornwallis. The officer was blindfolded and taken back to Washington's headquarters.

The British commander wanted to discuss the surrender terms with the American and French commanders. Messengers were sent back and forth between the two sides. Cornwallis proposed that his troops be allowed to return to Europe with the assurance that they would take no further part in the war. Washington rejected this proposal but agreed to a temporary truce while discussions were being held.

The negotiations, which took place in Moore House, a comfortable, private home behind the American lines, continued all day and well into the night on October 18. The Americans and French were represented by Colonel John Laurens and the Viscount de Noailles, Lafayette's brother-in-law. Representing the British were

< 43 >

Lieutenant Colonel Thomas Dundas and Major Alexander Ross. Washington reviewed the final surrender terms around midnight. They were then sent to Cornwallis, who was told to sign them by 11:00 the next morning. On October 19, just before 11:00, the agreement was returned bearing Cornwallis's signature.

According to the terms of the surrender, the British officers would be allowed to keep their weapons and personal belongings and to return to England with Cornwallis. The rank-and-file troops, however, would be held as prisoners in America for the remainder of the war. The agreement read, in part:

> The [British] garrison at York will march out to a place to be appointed in front of the posts, at two o'clock precisely with shouldered arms, colours [flags] cased, and drums beating a British or German march. They are then to ground their arms, and return to their encampments, where they will remain until they are dispatched to the places of their destination.[34]

The Surrender Ceremony

The surrender ceremony was held that afternoon on a field in front of Yorktown. The American army lined up on one side of the road that crossed the field, with Washington at its head. The French, led by Rochambeau, gathered along the opposite side.

The two victorious armies presented a sharp contrast in appearance. The French were elegant in their handsome uniforms. The infantry wore white coats with different colored lapels and collars according to their regiments. Artillerymen had gray coats that were trimmed with red velvet. Cavalrymen wore tall fur hats that had colored plumes, and their officers wore scarlet breeches (short pants that ended just below the knees) and blue coats. Few of the American soldiers, on the other hand, had uniforms. Washington and some

The surrender ceremony at Yorktown was held on October 19, 1781.

of the officers were dressed in the buff and blue colors of the Virginia militia, which Congress had adopted as the official uniform of the Continental Army in 1779. They were the exceptions, however. Most of the Americans, as a French officer noted, "were clad in small jackets of white cloth, dirty and ragged, and a number of them were almost barefoot."[35]

When the British army finally appeared, the soldiers marched slowly, with their band playing a wistful tune. General Cornwallis, who was ill, was not among his soldiers. Only about half his army was present. The sick and wounded men had remained in Yorktown. The infantry were wearing their famous red coats, while the artillerymen wore blue uniforms. According to an American army doctor, the British marched out of step and "were disorderly and unsoldierly."[36] Their officers, observed a New Jersey soldier, "behaved like boys who had been whipped at school."[37] Another American thought that many of the British were drunk.

The British soldiers, led by the second-in-command, General Charles O'Hara, passed, one by one, between the American and French troops to the spot where they were supposed to surrender

AFRICAN AMERICANS AT YORKTOWN

African Americans fought on both sides in the American Revolution. Historians estimate that as many as 5,000 African Americans fought on the American side during the war. Rhode Island had an all-black regiment in 1778, and black troops fought at Yorktown.

Free blacks enlisted, as did whites, for the adventure or because they believed in the American cause. Some African-American soldiers were runaway slaves. Others fought in exchange for their freedom.

One slave who worked at Cornwallis's headquarters was actually a spy for Lafayette. After the war, the Virginia legislature granted him his freedom, and he took the name "James Lafayette."

Blacks also fought on the British side. At the start of the war, the British encouraged slaves to join their side. Lord Dunmore, the Royal Governor of Virginia, proclaimed that all slaves "able and willing" to fight with the British would be given their freedom.[38] About 1,000 answered his call. Some of these soldiers ended up as free men in Canada, and others settled the British colony of Sierra Leone in Africa.

The British did not always treat the African Americans well who fought for them. Many were packed into camps where smallpox and other diseases were rampant and killed large numbers. At Yorktown, the American soldier Joseph Martin saw groups of black men lying in the woods, dead and dying. He said the British had abandoned them with "smallpox for their bounty and starvation and death for their wages."[39]

Just as whites did, black Americans fought, suffered, and died in the American Revolution. All who did so deserve to be remembered.

---

their weapons. The French band played various tunes, one of which was Yankee Doodle. "Many of the [British] soldiers," said the American doctor, "manifested a sullen temper, throwing their arms on the pile with violence."[40] General Benjamin Lincoln issued an order, and the ceremony was concluded in a more orderly fashion. A similar, smaller ceremony took place across the river at Gloucester Point.

< 46 >

Meanwhile, unknown to everyone at Yorktown, as the surrender ceremony was taking place, General Clinton and several thousand British troops in New York were setting sail at last to come to Cornwallis's aid. They arrived off the Virginia coast on October 24, but it was too late. The ships with their soldiers turned around and sailed back to New York.

The Aftermath and Significance of Yorktown

The day after the surrender ceremony, the American and French commanders entertained their British counterparts at dinner. Cornwallis remained in Yorktown, and was visited there by Rochambeau and Lafayette. That night, Washington sent a message to Congress:

> *I have the honor to inform Congress, that a Reduction of the British Army under the Command of Lord Cornwallis, is most happily effected. The unremitting Ardour which actuated every Officer and Soldier in the combined Army in this occasion, has principally led to this Important Event, at an earlier period than my most sanguine Hope had induced me to expect.*[41]

On October 21, the rank-and-file of the British army were marched off to prisoner-of-war camps in Virginia and Maryland. The officers were free to return to England.

Casualties and Other Losses

Losses at Yorktown were relatively light, especially when compared with battles of later wars. There were fewer casualties than in other battles of the American Revolution, such as those at Saratoga, Charleston, and Camden. At Yorktown, the British lost 156 men and 326 were wounded. Some of the 70 men counted as missing had

< 47 >

deserted the army. Among the Americans, 23 men were killed and 65 were wounded. The French lost 60 men and 134 were wounded.

The British surrendered more than 200 pieces of artillery, some 7,000 muskets and other small arms, 260 horses, and large amounts of ammunition and money. Moreover, over 7,000 troops were captured—about one third of all British forces in America.

Yorktown and the End of the War

When the British Prime Minister, Lord North, learned of the surrender at Yorktown a month later, he cried, "O God! It is all over!"[42] The war did not officially end, however, for almost two more years, and a number of minor military engagements would take place both on land and at sea. After Yorktown, the British still had troops in New York City, in Charleston, and at several locations in Georgia.

Yorktown, however, was the last major battle of the Revolution. Never again did the American army engage British troops. Yorktown convinced many British leaders that the war was not worth pursuing. In March 1782, King George III reluctantly appointed new ministers who were willing to consider American independence.

Peace talks began in April 1782. In October, the British accepted a preliminary agreement drafted by the Americans. The final treaty, called the Treaty of Paris, was signed a year later, on September 3, 1783. In this pact, Britain recognized the United States as an independent nation that extended from Canada to Florida (which Britain gave to Spain) and from the Atlantic Ocean to the Mississippi River. This was more territory than the U.S. government actually controlled at the war's end. Britain also agreed to withdraw all its forces from the United States. The treaty was ratified by Congress on January 14, 1784. The United States of America was recognized at last by Great Britain and by the rest of the world as a free and independent nation.

P A R T   T H R E E

HISTORY REMEMBERED

People interested in their nation's heritage enjoy visiting sites where history was made. Seeing the places where great events occurred, walking the grounds on which crucial battles were fought, and viewing the homes and buildings in which people of the past—those both great and ordinary—lived, worked, and died, help to bring history alive as nothing else can.

The United States has many agencies and organizations, both public and private, that are devoted to preserving these historic places. Several sites that relate to the battle of Yorktown, the life of George Washington, and early American history are located in eastern Virginia.

Colonial National Historical Park

The National Park Service, an agency of the U.S. government, manages Colonial National Historical Park. It consists of two neighboring sites: Yorktown, which includes both the town and surrounding battlefield areas, as well as the site of the first permanent English settlement at Jamestown. Colonial National Historical Park also includes the Cape Henry Memorial. This marks the approximate landing site of the first Jamestown colonists, who arrived in April 1607. The memorial also overlooks the waters where the French and British fleets fought the crucial naval battle that preceded the siege of Yorktown.

Location and Address Colonial National Historical Park, P.O. Box 210, Yorktown, VA 23690-0210. Telephone: (757) 898-3400.

Operating Hours All park grounds close daily at sunset, and are closed December 25. Yorktown Visitor Center: spring and fall 8:30 A.M.–5:00 P.M.; summer 8:30 A.M.–5:30 P.M.; winter 9:00 A.M.– 5:00 P.M. Jamestown Entrance Station: 8:30 A.M.–4:30 P.M. throughout the year. Jamestown Visitor Center: 9:00 A.M.–5:00 P.M. throughout the year.

< 49 >

A demonstration of battle tactics is staged during the Yorktown Victory Celebration each October.

Entrance Fees Yorktown: $4.00 per adult; children ages 16 and under admitted free. Admission includes all battlefield areas as well as Moore House and Nelson House in Yorktown. Jamestown: $5.00 per adult, children 16 and under free.

Special Events A number of special events are held at Colonial National Historical Park at Yorktown, including occasional artillery performances from April through October. The Yorktown Victory Celebration takes place every year on October 19, with a parade to mark the historic victory. On the weekend nearest that date, recreated 18th century military units present demonstrations of Revolutionary War tactics, and commemorative activities also take place.

From spring through fall, informal tours are given of the Nelson House, an early 18th century home that was hit by cannon fire. Beginning at 12:30 every day during the summer, a historical drama

< 51 >

is performed that reveals the Revolutionary War contributions of Thomas Nelson, Jr., who was commander of the Virginia militia during the siege at Yorktown.

Tours of the Moore House, where surrender negotiations took place, are provided on weekends in the spring and fall, and daily in the summer.

Yorktown

Yorktown itself is an active town with private homes and businesses. Most of the historic area, however, is protected by the National Park Service. This little town on the York River retains a few of the colonial dwellings that existed there at the time of the 1781 battle. Visitors can see the Moore House and the Nelson House. Poor Potter is the site of the largest pottery factory known to have existed in Colonial America. A walking tour of the village takes about 45 minutes.

Original and reconstructed fortifications may be seen on the battlefield. There are signs to indicate the location of British,

Dressed in period costume, groups of Jamestown "militiamen" fire cannons during reenactment exercises.

< 52 >

French, and American forces throughout the battle. Also preserved is the field on which the British forces surrendered. The Victory Monument, first authorized by the Continental Congress on October 29, 1781, was begun by the U.S. government in October 1881, for the 100th anniversary of the battle. Plaques on the monument grounds bear the names of Americans known to have lost their lives at Yorktown. Nearby, close to the French battery that fired first on the British, is another monument bearing the names of the French soldiers who died at Yorktown. A Visitor Center is located on the battlefield. There, one can find maps, displays, and other resources to aid in understanding the course and significance of the battle.

Jamestown Settlement

The state of Virginia maintains two living history museums, the Jamestown Settlement, and the Yorktown Victory Center near the National Park facilities.

Jamestown was the first permanent English colony in North America. Jamestown Settlement is a museum that is located about a mile from the original site. It is operated by the Jamestown-Yorktown Foundation. The settlement includes full-scale replicas of the three ships on which the first colonists arrived in 1607; a recreation of James Fort, which the colonists constructed on their arrival—the fort includes homes, a church, a storehouse, and an armory; and Powhatan Village, a recreated Native American community. Recently, archaeologists discovered the site of the original James Fort. Visitors can watch a 20-minute film, Jamestown: The Beginning, which tells the history of Jamestown. Visitors can tour the Old Towne (30-40 minutes), and the New Towne (45 minutes) daily except Christmas, to learn about life in Jamestown—from its earliest days to the late 1600s.

The Yorktown Victory Center's Living History Museum provides a first-hand look at colonial life in America.

Location and Address   Jamestown-Yorktown Foundation, P.O. Box 1607, Williamsburg, VA 23187. Telephone: (757) 253-4838.

Operating Hours   9:00 A.M.–5:00 P.M. daily except Christmas Day and New Year's Day.

Entrance Fees $9.75 per adult; $4.75 children 12 and under; educational groups admitted free of charge with a written fee waiver.

Exhibits   Three exhibits display artifacts of the period, such as English navigational instruments; Native American clothing; stones and other remains of the original Jamestown settlement. The displays illuminate the factors that led to the English colonization of the New World, the technological innovations that made possible long ocean voyages to new destinations, and the history of Native Americans in Virginia before the English arrived.

Special Events   Interpreters dressed in historic costumes lead visitors in hands-on demonstrations of various activities, such as militia drills, cooking, and tool-making, using techniques and tools that accurately reflect the time period.

< 54 >

Colonial Williamsburg

About 15 to 20 minutes from both Yorktown and Jamestown by car is Colonial Williamsburg, which is run by the Colonial Williamsburg Foundation. Colonial Williamsburg is a 173-acre working town. Visitors can meet and talk with people there who dress, live, and work as if they were in 18th-century America. The town has more than 500 buildings that may be visited, including the Governor's Palace, Bruton Parish Church, the Courthouse, the state Capitol building, and restaurants that serve food of the period. The Visitor Center shows *Williamsburg—The Story of a Patriot*, a 35-minute film about the dramatic events in Virginia that led up to the American Revolution.

Two museums adjoin the Colonial Williamsburg area. The DeWitt Wallace Decorative Arts Gallery holds a large collection of American and English antiques. The Abby Aldrich Rockefeller Folk Art Center houses a fine collection of American folk art. Also nearby is Bassett Hall, an 18th century frame house, which was for many years the Williamsburg home of Mr. and Mrs. John D. Rockefeller, Jr., the founders of Colonial Williamsburg.

Eight miles southeast of Colonial Williamsburg, on the James River, is Carter's Grove plantation, which dates from the 1600s. Its

The armory in Colonial Williamsburg was used to store the guns and ammunition of the Virginia militia.

Visitors to Colonial Williamsburg are encouraged to try their hand at cooking using colonial techniques.

mansion has been called "the most beautiful house in America." The grounds include the reconstructed 18th century slave quarters. Also located on the grounds are the partially reconstructed settle ment and fort of Wolstenholme Towne, home of the area's first settlers, and the Winthrop Rockefeller Archaeology Museum.

Location and Address Colonial Williamsburg Foundation, P.O. Box 1776, Williamsburg, VA 23187-1776. Telephone: 1-800-HISTORY.

Operating Hours Colonial Williamsburg is open 9:00 A.M.– 5:30 P.M. seven days a week, 365 days a year.

Entrance Fees The Basic Ticket, which is good for one day and includes admission to a number of different exhibits, costs $25 for adults, $15 for children ages 6 to 12, and is free for children under 6. Other ticket combinations are also available.

Special Events The Grand Illumination, which takes place in December, is a 62-year-old tradition at Colonial Williamsburg, attracting thousands of visitors. At the signal of a cannon blast,

< 56 >

candles are lit in the windows of homes, shops, and public buildings throughout the Historic Area. The illumination is followed by fireworks, singing, dancing, and outdoor music performances.

Historic Places in the Life of George Washington

A few hours drive north of Yorktown are two historic places in the life of George Washington.

George Washington Birthplace National Monument

The National Park Service maintains this 538-acre site in Westmoreland County on the Potomac River, 38 miles east of Fredericksburg, Virginia. Washington lived there with his family until the age of three. The monument includes the birthplace home site, the colonial farm, and the family burial grounds.

Location and Address George Washington Birthplace National Monument, Rural Route 1, Box 717, Washington's Birthplace, VA 22443. Telephone: (804) 224-1732.

Operating Hours Daily, 9:00 A.M.–5:00 P.M., except Christmas Day and New Year's Day.

Entrance Fees $2.00 per person, age 17 years and older.

Exhibits These include a history of the Washington family, displays of Washington family artifacts, and a 14-minute film about the National Monument.

Special Events George Washington's Birthday is celebrated annually on President's Day and on his actual date of birth (February 22) with special colonial activities throughout the day.

Mount Vernon

Mount Vernon, on the Potomac River about 16 miles south of Washington, D.C., was Washington's home for most of his life. He

< 57 >

acquired it in 1754, at age 22, and died there in 1799. His widow Martha lived at Mount Vernon until she died in 1802. Both are buried on the grounds.

Washington's home at Mount Vernon is open to visitors.

Mount Vernon is managed by the Mount Vernon Ladies' Association. It consists of the mansion, gardens, family tomb, and outbuildings that include the slave quarters. A museum displays many of the Washingtons' personal possessions such as combs, brushes, clothing, furniture, and kitchen equipment, as well as paintings and sculptures.

Location and Address Mount Vernon Ladies' Association, Mount Vernon, VA 22121. Telephone: (703) 780-2000.

Operating Hours 9:00 A.M.–5:00 P.M.; summer, 8:00 A.M.–5:00 P.M.

Entrance Fees $8.00 general admission for adults; $7.50 for seniors; $4.00 for children ages 6 to 11; children under age 6 free.

Exhibits The newest exhibit at Mount Vernon, "George Washington: Pioneer Farmer," features Washington's agricultural innovations. The 4-acre exhibition site runs along the Potomac River and includes demonstrations of period farming.

Special Events Washington's birthday and Independence Day (July 4) are both celebrated at Mount Vernon. Admission is free on Washington's birthday, and a parade is held by the U.S. Army Fife and Drum Corps. On July 4, patriotic music is performed at the site.

CHRONOLOGY OF THE REVOLUTIONARY WAR

September 1774	First Continental Congress meets in Philadelphia.
April 1775	British army and the Massachusetts militia fight at Lexington and Concord near Boston.
May 1775	Massachusetts and Vermont militias capture Fort Ticonderoga on Lake Champlain in New York.
June 1775	Second Continental Congress appoints Washington commander of the Continental Army.
June 1775	Americans fight at the Battle of Bunker Hill.
August 1775–July 1776	American attempts to invade Canada fail.
March 1776	British evacuate Boston for New York.
July 1776	Continental Congress declares the United States independent from Great Britain.
August–November 1776	British under General Howe drive Washington's army out of New York.
December 1776	Washington defeats the British at Trenton, New Jersey.
January 1777	Washington defeats the British at Princeton, New Jersey.
June–October 1777	British General Burgoyne's invasion of New York fails; he surrenders at Saratoga to Horatio Gates.
September–October 1777	Howe defeats Washington at Brandywine and Germantown, Pennsylvania, and occupies Philadelphia.
Winter 1777-78	Continental Army at Valley Forge
February 1778	France and the United States form an alliance.

< 59 >

June 1778	British leave Philadelphia for New York; Washington battles them at Monmouth Courthouse, New Jersey.
July 1778	General Clark captures British posts in the Northwest.
December 1779	British capture Savannah, Georgia.
February–May 1780	British besiege and capture Charleston, South Carolina.
July 1780	4,000 French troops under Rochambeau arrive at Newport, Rhode Island.
August 1780	British under Cornwallis defeat Americans under Gates at Camden, South Carolina.
September 1780	American General Benedict Arnold commits treason and joins the British.
January–March 1781	Nathanael Greene battles Cornwallis in the Carolinas.
January–May 1781	Mutinies occur in the Continental Army.
April 1781	Cornwallis marches from North Carolina to Virginia.
May–August 1781	Cornwallis spars with Lafayette in Virginia and fortifies Yorktown.
August 1781	Washington and Rochambeau march south to join Lafayette and trap Cornwallis at Yorktown.
September–October 1781	Siege of Yorktown
September 1781	French fleet under De Grasse defeats British under Graves in Chesapeake Bay.
October 1781	Cornwallis surrenders at Yorktown.
April 1782	Peace talks begin in Paris between Britain and the United States.
September 1783	Treaty of Paris signed, ending the American Revolution.

FURTHER READING

Dolan, Edward F. *The American Revolution: How We Fought the War of Independence.* Brookfield, CT: Millbrook, 1995.

Gay, Kathlyn, and Martin Gay. *Revolutionary War.* New York: Twenty-First Century Books, 1995.

Hakim, Joy. *A History of US: From Colonies to Country.* New York: Oxford, 1983.

Kent, Zachary. *The Surrender at Yorktown.* Chicago: Childrens Press, 1989.

Martin, Albert. *The War for Independence: The Story of the American Revolution.* New York: Atheneum, 1988.

Murphy, Jim. *A Young Patriot: The American Revolution as Experienced by One Boy.* Boston: Clarion, 1996.

Steins, Richard. *A Nation Is Born: Rebellion & Independence in America.* New York: Twenty-First Century Books, 1993.

WEB SITES

For more information about Colonial National Historical Park, visit its web site at:

http://www.nps.gov/colo

The history of the Yorktown village comes alive at:

http://www.williamsburg.com/york/york.html

   This site provides information on special events at Yorktown, as well as on area dining, shopping, hotels, and camping.

Learn more about the history of Jamestown, its original settlers, and current events there at:

http:www.williamsburg.com/james/james.html

Plan a trip to Colonial Williamsburg by visiting it online at:
http://www.williamsburg.com/wol/wol.html

The George Washington Birthplace National Memorial maintains a site that provides information about the park's attractions, services, and programs. Visit it at:

http://www.nps.gov/gewa

Visit Mount Vernon online to take a tour of Mount Vernon, view its library collections, or find other educational resources:

http://www.mountvernon.org

SOURCE NOTES

Part One

1. Otis's remarks were heard by John Adams, who recorded them years later. Adams's recollections are in L. Kinvin Wroth and Hiller B. Zobel, eds., *Legal Papers of John Adams,* vol. 2 (Cambridge, MA: Harvard University Press, 1965), pp. 106–147.

2. Quoted in Robert Middlekauf, *The Glorious Cause: The American Revolution, 1763–1789* (New York: Oxford University Press, 1982), p. 114.

3. Ibid., p. 262.

4. Quoted in Allen French, *General Gage's Informers* (New York: Greenwood Press, 1968), p. 31.

5. Quoted in Middlekauf, *The Glorious Cause,* p. 325.

6. Samuel Eliot Morison, *The Oxford History of the American People* (New York: Oxford University Press, 1965), p. 224.

7. Quoted in Christopher Hibbert, *Rebels and Redcoats: The American Revolution through British Eyes* (New York: W. W. Norton, 1990), p. 142.

8. Henry Steele Commager and Richard B. Morris, eds., *The Spirit of Seventy-Six* (New York: Harper & Row, 1958), p. 645.

9. Ibid., p. 640.

10. Quoted in Page Smith, *A New Age Now Begins: A People's History of the American Revolution,* vol. 2 (New York: McGraw-Hill, 1976), p. 1390.

11. Quoted in John Keegan, *Fields of Battle: The Wars for North America* (New York: Alfred A. Knopf, 1995), p. 178.

12. Quoted in Hibbert, *Rebels and Redcoats,* p. 315.

< 62 >

Part Two

1. Quoted in Smith, *A New Age Now Begins*, pp. 1646-1647.
2. Ibid., p. 1639.
3. Quoted in Burke Davis, *The Campaign That Won America: The Story of Yorktown* (New York: Dial Press, 1970), p. 3.
4. Quoted in Robert Leckie, *George Washington's War: The Saga of the American Revolution* (New York: HarperCollins, 1992), p. 634.
5. Quoted in Smith, *A New Age Now Begins*, p. 1654.
6. Quoted in James Flexner, *Washington: The Indispensable Man* (Boston: Little, Brown, 1974), p. 157.
7. Letter of Jan. 2, 1814, to Dr. Walter Jones, in *The Life and Selected Writings of Thomas Jefferson*, eds. Adrienne Koch and William Peden (New York: Modern Library, 1944), p. 174.
8. Quoted in Smith, *A New Age Now Begins*, p. 974.
9. Ibid., p. 976.
10. Quoted in Davis, *The Campaign That Won America*, p. 14.
11. Quoted in Smith, *A New Age Now Begins*, p. 1659.
12. Ibid., p. 1663.
13. Ibid., p. 1666.
14. Ibid., p. 1668.
15. Ibid., p. 1669.
16. Quoted in Davis, *The Campaign That Won America*, pp. 174–175.
17. Ibid., p. 169.
18. Ibid., p. 136.
19. Ibid., p. 140.
20. Ibid., p. 138.
21. Ibid., p. 201.
22. Ibid., p. 205.
23. Quoted in Smith, *A New Age Now Begins*, p. 1699.
24. Quoted in Davis, *The Campaign That Won America*, p. 218.
25. Quoted in Smith, *A New Age Now Begins*, p. 1700.
26. Quoted in Davis, *The Campaign That Won America*, p. 221.
27. Ibid., p. 224.
28. Ibid., p. 234.
29. Ibid., p. 235.

< 63 >

30. Ibid., p. 236.
31. Ibid., p. 237.
32. Ibid., p. 256.
33. Ibid.
34. Quoted in Smith, *A New Age Now Begins*, pp. 1705–1706.
35. Quoted in Davis, *The Campaign That Won America*, p. 264.
36. Quoted in Smith, *A New Age Now Begins*, p. 1707.
37. Quoted in Davis, *The Campaign That Won America*, p. 266.
38. Quoted in Commager, *The Spirit of Seventy-Six*, p. 111.
39. Quoted in Smith, *A New Age Now Begins*, pp. 1696–1697.
40. Ibid., p. 1707.
41. Quoted in Davis, *The Campaign That Won America*, p. 276.
42. Quoted in Hubbard Cobb, *America's Battlefields: A Complete Guide to the Historic Conflicts in Words, Maps, and Photos* (New York: Macmillan, 1995), p. 94.

OTHER SOURCES

Boatner III, Mark M. *Encyclopedia of the American Revolution.* Bicentennial Edition. New York: McKay, 1976.

Greene, Jack P., and J. R. Pole, eds. *The Blackwell Encyclopedia of the American Revolution.* Cambridge, MA: Blackwell, 1991.

Purcell, L. Edward, and David F. Burg, eds. *The World Almanac of the American Revolution.* New York: World Almanac, 1992.

Stokesbury, James L. *A Short History of the American Revolution.* New York: Morrow, 1991.

Wood, W. J. *Battles of the Revolutionary War, 1775-1781.* Chapel Hill, NC: Algonquin Books, 1990.

INDEX

J
973.337   Weber, Michael,
W   1945-
    Yorktown.

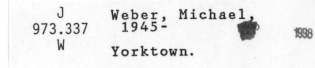

$20.40

DATE			